CONTENTS

Tracking, mixing, and mastering by Jake Johnson
Drums by Scott Schroedl
Guitars by Doug Boduch
Bass by Tom McGirr
Keyboards by Warren Wiegratz

ISBN 978-1-4234-0424-0424-8

Visit Hal Leonard Online at www.halleonard.com

HAL•LEONARD®
CORPORATION
7777 W. BLUEMOUND RD. P.O. BOX 13819
MILWAUKEE, WISCONSIN 53213

Barracuda

Words and Music by Nancy Wilson, Ann Wilson, Michael Derosier and Roger Fisher

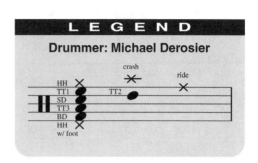

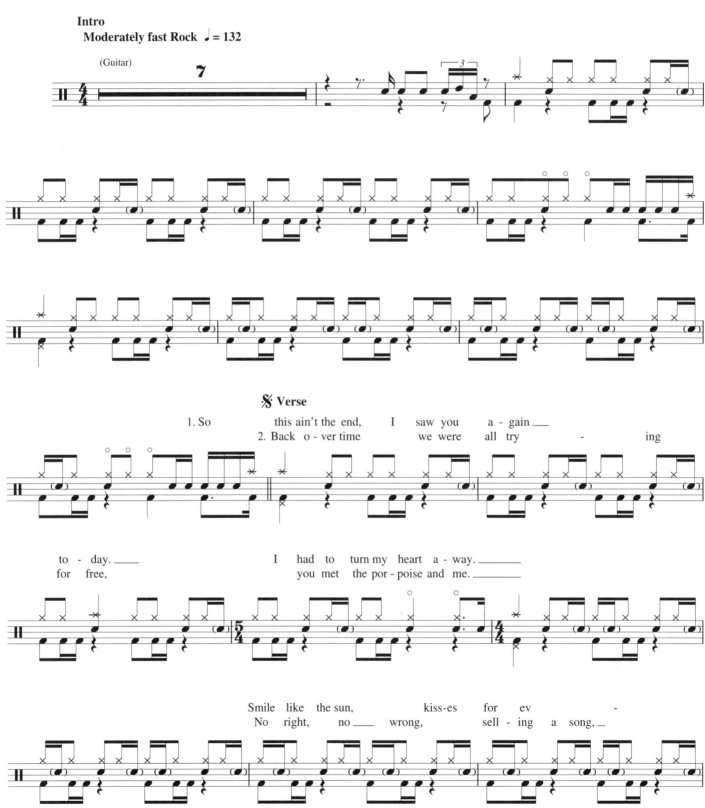

All that night and all the next swam with-out look-ing back,

made for the west-ern pools. Sil - ly, sil - ly fools.

Guitar Solo

The

Chorus

real thing don't do the trick, ___ no, you bet - ter make up some - thing _ quick. ___

___ You gon - na burn, burn, _ burn, ___ burn, burn _ it to the

wick. ___ Oh, _____

___ bar - ra - bar - ra - cu - da. Yeah.

Outro

Come Together

Words and Music by John Lennon and Paul McCartney

Intro
Moderately slow Rock ♩ = 82

Shoot me.   Shoot me.

Shoot me.   Shoot me.

Verse
1. Here come ol' flat-top, he come groov-in' up slow-ly, he got Joo Joo eye-ball, he one

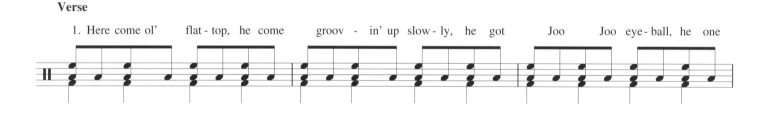

ho - ly roll - er. He got hair _ down _ to _ his knee,

got to be a jok - er, he just do what he please. _ Shoot me.

Shoot me.   Shoot me.

Outro

Mississippi Queen

Words and Music by Leslie West, Felix Pappalardi, Corky Laing and David Rea

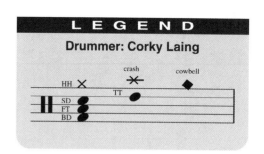

Intro
Half-time feel
Moderately ♩ = 140

Chorus

Mis - sis - sip - pi   Queen, ____

do   you   know ____   what   I   mean?   Mis -

sis - sip - pi   Queen, ____   she taught me   ev - 'ry - thing.

Verse

1. Way   down ____   a - round   Vicks - burg,   a - round Lou -

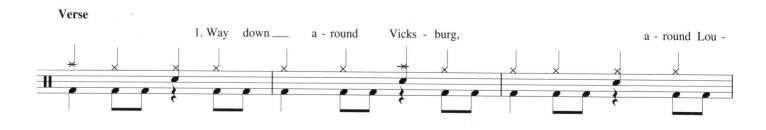

Verse

2. This la - dy she __ asked me   if I would

be her man. __   You know __ that I   told her   I'd __ do __

__ what I   can   to keep __ her look - in' pret - ty.

Buy   her dress - es that   shine. While the   rest of them   dudes   was a

mak - in' their   bread;   bud - dy, beg your par - don I was   los - in' mine.

Guitar Solo

Outro

You know _

_ she was a danc - er, _____   she moved _ bet - ter on wine. While the

rest of them _ dudes _ was _ get - tin' their kicks;   broth - er, beg your par - don, I was

get - tin' mine, _____   Hey, _____ Mis - sis - sip - pi Queen. _

Radar Love

Words and Music by George Kooymans and Barry Hay

1. I been driv -

Verse

- in' all night, __ my hand's wet on the wheel.

There's a voice __ in my head __ that drives my heel. __

It's my ba - by call - in', says, "I

need __ you here." __ And it's a

half past four and I'm shift - in' gear. _____

Pre-Chorus

When she is lone - ly and ___ the long -

- ing gets too much, ___ she sends a ca -

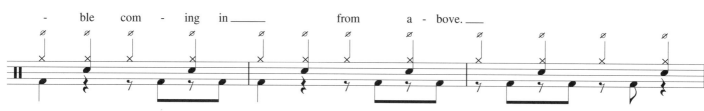

- ble com - ing in ___ from a - bove. ___

Don't need a phone at all. ___

Chorus

We've got a thing, ___

___ and that's a called ra - dar love. ___

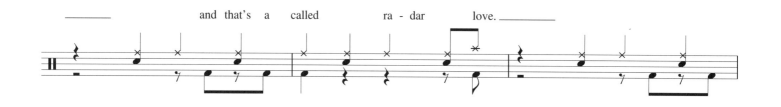

We've got a wave ___ in the air. ___

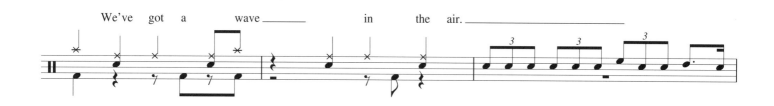

Interlude

Ra - dar love. ___

Verse

2. The ra - di - o's play - in' some for - got - ten song. ___

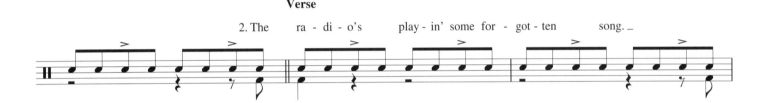

Bren - da Lee ___

com - in' on strong. _____ The

road has got ___ me hyp - no - tized, _____

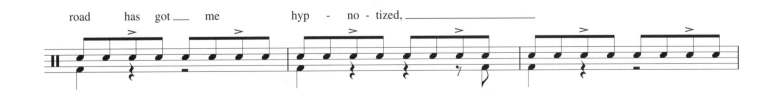

and I'm spin-nin' in-to ___ a new ___ sun - rise. _____

___ **Pre-Chorus**

When I ___ get lone -

- ly and I'm sure I've had e - nough, ___

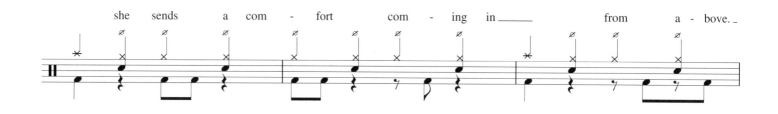

she sends a com - fort com - ing in ___ from a - bove. _

___ We don't need no let - ter at all. _____

Chorus

We've got a thing _____ that's called ra - dar love. _

_____ We've got a light _____ in the sky. _

Interlude

Ra - dar   love. __

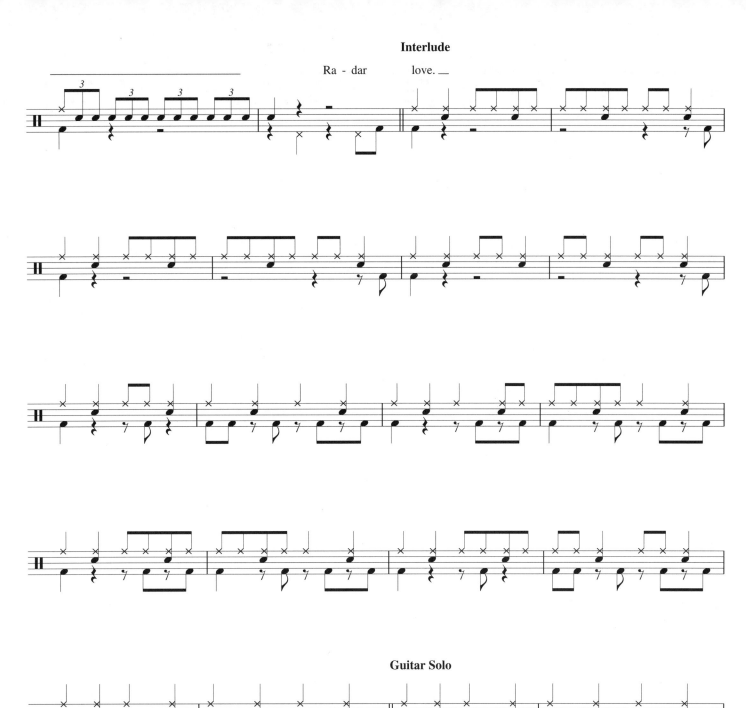

Guitar Solo

22

Breakdown

Interlude

Woo!

Verse

3. No more speed, I'm al-most there. _

Got-ta keep cool, now, got-ta take care. _____

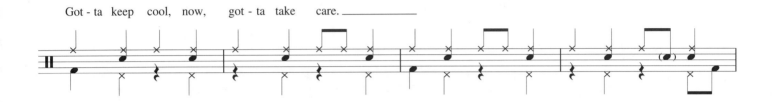

Last car to pass, here I go! _ And the

line of cars_ drove down real slow, whoa. _ And the

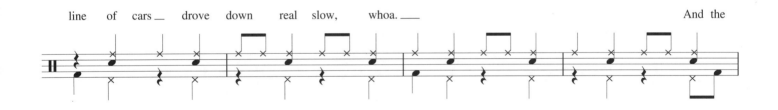

ra-di-o played that for-got-ten song. _

Bren-da Lee's _ com-in' on strong. _____ And the

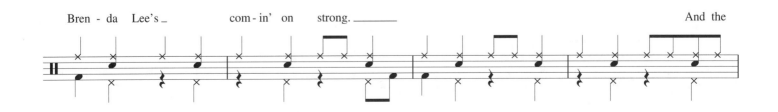

news man sang his ___ theme song. _ Oh, ___

one more ra - dar lov - er gone. _____

Pre-Chorus

When I ___ get lone - ly and I'm sure I've had e - nough,

___ she sends a com - fort com - ing in ___ from a - bove. _

___ We don't need no let - ter at all. ___

Chorus

We've _____ got a thing _____ that's called _ ra - dar love. ___

We've _____ got a light _____ in the sky. _____

Space Truckin'

Words and Music by Ritchie Blackmore, Ian Gillan,
Roger Glover, Jon Lord and Ian Paice

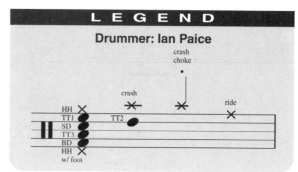

Guitar Solo

Space truck-in'.

Drum Solo

*Overdubbed drum break. (Snares off, next 17 meas.)

**Play with one stick while other stick presses into head to deaden and raise pitch.

32

Interlude

Come

Chorus

on!   Come   on!   Come   on!   Let's

go   space   truck - in'.   Come   on!   Come   on!   Come

Outro

on!   Space   truck - in'.   Yeah, ___ yeah, _   yeah, _

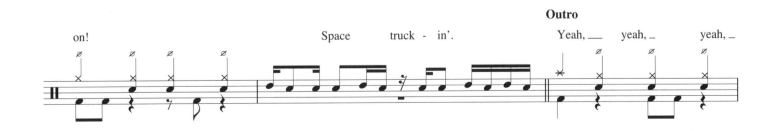

Won't Get Fooled Again

Words and Music by Pete Townshend

Chorus

cide   and   the shot - gun   sings   the   song. __

I'll   tip   my   hat   to   the   new   con - sti - tu - tion,

take   a   bow __   for the new rev - o - lu - tion.   Smile and   grin __   at the

change   all a - round,   pick up my gui - tar   and play, __

just   like   yes - ter - day, __   then I'll get on   my knees and

pray _____   we

don't   get fooled __ a - gain. _____

Chorus

Bridge

move my - self and my fam -'ly a - side, _____ if we hap - pen to be

left half _ a - live. _ I'll get all my pa - pers and smile _ at the sky, oh, I

know that the hyp - no - tized nev - er lie.

Do   ya?

Guitar Solo

Yeah!   3. There's

Verse
noth - ing   in   the   street ___   looks   an - y   dif - fer - ent   to   me, _

___   and the   slo - gans   are   re - placed ___   by ___   the   by. ___

___   And   the   part - ing   on   the   left _

___   is   now   part - ing   on   the   right, ___   and the

beards   have   all ___ grown   long - er   o - ver - night. _____

Chorus
I'll   tip   my   hat   to   the   new   con - sti - tu -   tion,

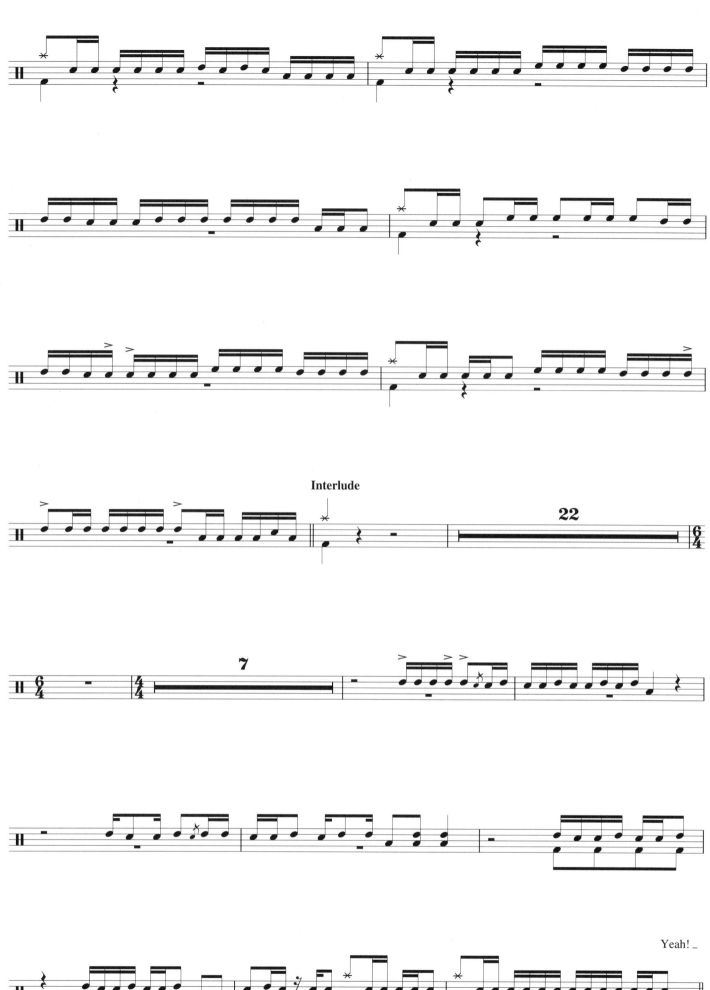

Interlude

22

7

Yeah! _

Outro

Meet   the   new ___ boss.   Same   as   the   old   boss.

Free time

Walk This Way

Words and Music by Steven Tyler and Joe Perry

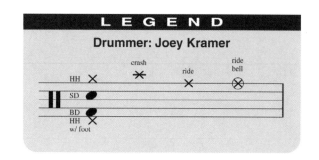

Intro
Moderate Rock ♩ = 120

Verse

1. Back-stroke lov-er al-ways hid-in' 'neath the cov-ers, "Gon-na talk to you," my dad-dy say,_ said, "You

ain't seen noth-in' till you're down on a muf-fin, then you're sure to be a chang-in' your ways."_ I met a

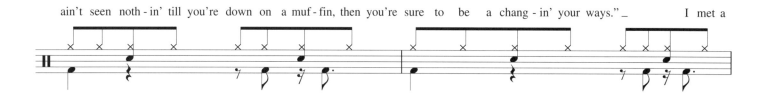

cheer-lead-er, was a real young bleed-er all the times I could rem-i-nisce,_ 'cause the

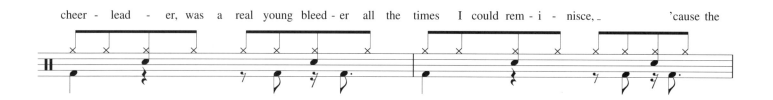

best things in lov-in' with a sis-ter and a cou-sin on-ly start-ed with a lit-tle kiss,_ a like this!

Interlude

Verse

2., 4. See - saw swing-in' with the boys in the school and your feet fly-in' up in the air, __ I sing,

"Hey did-dle did-dle" with your kit-ty in the mid-dle of the swing like you did-n't care. __ So I

took a big chance at the high school dance with a miss-y who was read-y to play, __ was a

me she was fool-in' 'cause she knew what she was do-in' { and I know'd love was here to stay __ when she told me to...}
{ when she told me how to walk this way. __ She told __ me to...}

To Coda ⊕

 Chorus

(Walk this __ way, __ talk this __ way, __ { walk } this __ way, __
{ talk }

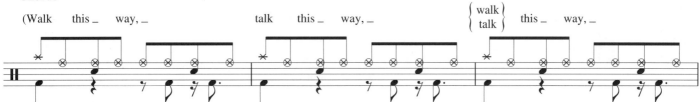

Guitar Solo

Uh, just gim - me a kiss. _____

walk this __ way.) ___

47

A like this!

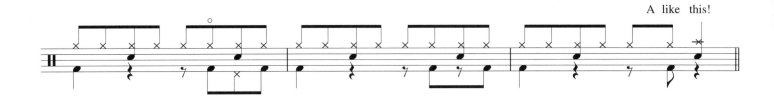

Interlude

Oo.   Uh.

Verse

3. School girl skin-ny with a class-y kind-a sas-sy lit-tle skirts climb-in' way up her knee,___   there was

three young lad-ies in the school gym lock-er when I   no-ticed they was look-in' at   me. ___   I was a

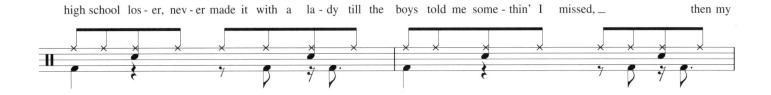

high school los-er, nev-er made it with a   la-dy till the boys told me some-thin' I   missed, ___   then my

D.S. al Coda

next door neigh-bor with a daugh-ter had a fa-vor so I   gave her just a   lit-tle   kiss___ a like this!

Coda

talk   this ___ way, ___   talk   this ___ way, ___

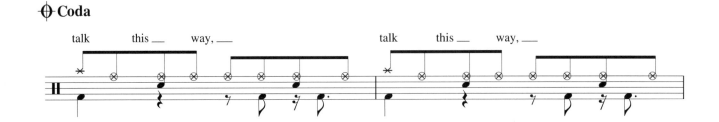

White Room

Words and Music by Jack Bruce and Pete Brown

D.C. al Coda
(take repeat)

Begin fade

Fade out

HAL·LEONARD DRUM PLAY·ALONG™

Play your favorite songs quickly and easily with the *Drum Play-Along™* series. Just follow the drum notation, listen to the CD to hear how the drums should sound, then play along using the separate backing tracks. The lyrics are also included for quick reference. The audio CD is playable on any CD player. For PC and Mac computer users, the CD is enhanced so you can adjust the recording to any tempo without changing the pitch!

Book/CD Packs

VOLUME 1 – POP/ROCK
Hurts So Good • Message in a Bottle • No Reply at All • Owner of a Lonely Heart • Peg • Rosanna • Separate Ways (Worlds Apart) • Swingtown.
00699742 Book/CD Pack $12.95

VOLUME 2 – CLASSIC ROCK
Barracuda • Come Together • Mississippi Queen • Radar Love • Space Truckin' • Walk This Way • White Room • Won't Get Fooled Again.
00699741 Book/CD Pack $12.95

VOLUME 3 – HARD ROCK
Bark at the Moon • Detroit Rock City • Living After Midnight • Panama • Rock You like a Hurricane • Run to the Hills • Smoke on the Water • War Pigs (Interpolating Luke's Wall).
00699743 Book/CD Pack $12.95

VOLUME 4 – MODERN ROCK
Chop Suey! • Duality • Here to Stay • Judith • Nice to Know You • Nookie • One Step Closer • Whatever.
00699744 Book/CD Pack $12.95

VOLUME 5 – FUNK
Cissy Strut • Cold Sweat, Part 1 • Fight the Power, Part 1 • Flashlight • Pick Up the Pieces • Shining Star • Soul Vaccination • Superstition.
00699745 Book/CD Pack $12.95

Prices, contents and availability subject to change without notice and may vary outside the US.